THE DALAI LAMA

by Christopher Gibb

OTHER TITLES IN THE SERIES
Louis Braille by Beverley Birch (1-85015-139-3)
Marie Curie by Beverley Birch (1-85015-092-3)
Father Damien by Pam Brown (1-85015-084-2)
Henry Dunant by Pam Brown (1-85015-106-7)
Mahatma Gandhi by Michael Nicholson (1-85015-091-5)
Bob Geldof by Charlotte Gray (1-85015-085-0)
Martin Luther King by Valerie Schloredt and Pam Brown
    (1-85015-086-9)
Florence Nightingale by Pam Brown (1-85015-117-2)
Louis Pasteur by Beverley Birch (1-85015-140-7)
Albert Schweitzer by James Bentley (1-85015-114-8)
Sir Peter Scott by Julia Courtney (1-85015-108-3)
Mother Teresa by Charlotte Gray (1-85015-093-1)
Desmond Tutu by David Winner (1-85015-087-7)
Lech Walesa by Mary Craig (1-85015-107-5)
Raoul Wallenberg by Michael Nicholson and
    David Winner (1-85015-109-1)
Coming Soon
Robert Baden Powell by Julia Courtney (1-85015-180-6)
Charlie Chaplin by Pam Brown (1-85015-143-1)
Maria Montessori by Michael Pollard (1-85015-156-3)

Picture Credits
Camera Press: 31, China Photo Service 46, Adrian Cowell 22, 34, 50, 51 (top), Ann Hutchison 6-7, Guy Newcombe 59; ETV Ltd: 43; Christopher Gibb: 44-5, 47, 48; Robert Harding Picture Library: 19, 33, Nigel Blake 16 (top), Nigel Blythe 36-7; Michael Holford: 58; Hutchinson Library: 18 (top), Felix Greene 12 (below), Sarah Hartington 44 (below); The India Office: 12-13; Paul Popper Ltd: 39, 40, 53, 57, © Daily Mail 41; Remote Source: 8-9; Rex Features: cover, 4; Frederick Spencer Chapman: 10, 11, 15, 16 (below), 18 (below), 20, 21, 23, 24, 29; Spencer Chapman Collection 35; Dr. Tedeus Skorupski: 51 (below), 54 (below), 55; Tibet Photo Archive: 63. Map on page 26 drawn by Geoffrey Pleasance.

The Publishers would like to thank Faith Spencer Chapman for her most generous assistance on this book and Simon Normanton for sharing his picture research information.

Published in Great Britain in 1990
by Exley Publications Ltd,
16 Chalk Hill, Watford,
Herts WD1 4BN, United Kingdom.

Copyright © Exley Publications, 1990

British Library Cataloguing in Publication Data
Gibb, Christopher, 1955-.
    The Dalai Lama —
    (People who have helped the world).
    1. Tibet. Bstan-dzin-ryga-mtsho,
    Dalai Lama XIV, 1935-
    I. Title.
    II. Series.
    951'.5042'0924

ISBN 1-85015-141-5

Series conceived and edited by Helen Exley
Picture research: Diana Briscoe.
Editorial: Margaret Montgomery.
Glossary: Samantha Armstrong.
Typeset by Brush Off Studios, St Albans.
Printed and bound in Hungary.

THE DALAI LAMA

The leader of the exiled people of Tibet – and patient worker for world peace

Christopher Gibb

EXLEY

"The laughing Buddha"

"Do you think that Buddhism is 'best'?" asked somebody from the audience during a talk the Dalai Lama gave in London in 1988. His Holiness laughed, and replied that the Dalai Lama was likely to think that Buddhism was best – but it was only best for him, and something else could be best for somebody else.

There are some people who make you laugh and smile all the time, not just with jokes but with their own *joie de vivre*. When asked a more complicated question on Buddhist philosophy at that same meeting, the Dalai Lama cocked his head, wearing an expression which clearly said, "You don't expect me to answer that question do you?" And then he launched into a clear and closely-argued line of reasoning which held the hall spellbound. When he had finished, his face lit up with a mischievous grin, "Well that's what I think anyway" he said, as though what he had just talked about was something any-one could have thought of. No wonder he is known as "the laughing Buddha".

And yet, seldom has a person had more cause to lament the lot that fate has heaped upon him and his people. Once the ruler of Tibet, a country the size of western Europe, Tenzin Gyatso, His Holiness the fourteenth Dalai Lama, is now an exile in India, along with one hundred thousand other Tibetans.

From exile, over the last thirty years he has had to watch the Chinese systematically attempt to stamp out the rich and ancient culture of Tibet. He has had to witness the massacre, imprisonment and degradation of his people, and the suppression of Buddhism – the very life blood of his country.

"Respect seems natural when you meet him [the Dalai Lama], but it is not awe. You can talk with him, and laugh with him, and discuss things with him, and although the underlying respect remains it is like being in the presence of a very old and warm friend."

Roger Hicks and Ngakpa Chogyam, from their biography, "Great Ocean".

5

TIBET

An international figure

But despite all this suffering, and perhaps in some ways because of it, the Dalai Lama has become a truly international figure. He has not become, as so many other exiled leaders have, a weapon used in the constant war of words between East and West – communism versus capitalism. Instead he is someone who preaches compassion and peace for *all* peoples. Although his philosophy, and indeed serenity, derive from his exhaustive following and study of Tibetan Buddhism, the Dalai Lama is no dogmatist – as he has shown in many of his speeches. Indeed, he goes out of his way to stress the underlying similarity of all religions. His themes are the universal responsibility we all have to develop. They are "a good heart"; the need for

Collecting water in the squalor of one of the first Tibetan refugee camps set up in New Delhi, India, in 1959. The camps were set up by India as a place to live for all the Tibetan people driven out of their homeland and forced to live in exile. Due to the great generosity of the Indian government and the industry of the refugees themselves, most Tibetan settlements in India have greatly improved since the early days. Today, there are schools, hospitals and monasteries – but it isn't home.

compassion – particularly as the means to achieve peace in this world; and the way religion – any religion – can be used as a tool to achieve greater happiness for ourselves and others.

There are lessons in his words for us all.

Today, Tenzin Gyatso, the fourteenth Dalai Lama of Tibet, has become one of the world's most respected leaders. Wherever he travels, he is invited by world leaders to talk to them about world peace and their country's problems. He lectures widely and has a worldwide influence.

He quietly, gently repeats the most simple, the most obvious principles. But his message reaches through. Wherever he goes, people seem to laugh. He definitely has a rare charisma – and therefore an influence that is far beyond his position as the

exiled leader of Tibet.

Perhaps his secret is that he cuts across religious, national and political barriers and reaches the hearts of human beings. He truly cares for all peoples, and everything he does is for the sake of promoting peace in this world. This can only be done, he argues, when we as individuals take a closer look at ourselves and recognize that, above all, we are all members of the same human family.

"We need a revolution," he says, "in our commitment to humanitarian values."

The forbidden land

Tibet is a vast and beautiful country. It is bounded on three sides by some of the highest mountains in the world – the rugged Karakorams and Ladakh

mountains in the West, the wild and remote Chang Tang ranges to the North, and the great rock barrier of the Himalayas that runs for 2,400 kilometres along Tibet's southern border. No wonder Tibet has been called the "Roof of the World", for the average height of the land is around 4,500 metres.

In the past, Tibet's encircling mountains have acted like a kind of fortress. Conquering armies were dismayed by the soaring mountain precipices, the bitter winds and snow, and the absence of roads. Even in the East where the land is lower, the country is rugged and barren and the distances are enormous – it is over 1,200 kilometres from the capital, Lhasa, to the Chinese frontier. This was one of the reasons why the way of life of the people remained so little changed for hundreds of years. In addition Tibetans discouraged all foreign influence; Tibet

Looking south from the high Tibetan plateau to the north face of Mount Everest and the soaring peaks of the Himalayas. Protected by the highest natural barrier in the world, Tibetan society and religion was able to develop in its own unique way, without interference from all but the hardiest outsiders.

was known as the "Forbidden Land". Its isolation also contributed to its unique religious culture.

For at the time of the present Dalai Lama's birth in 1935, Tibet was still essentially a feudal society. Nearly half the population lived as wandering nomads, particularly in the wild Amdo and Kham regions of north-east Tibet. Most of the richest farmland was owned by the great monasteries and the nobility. On these great estates peasants might own a plot of land for their own use, but they also had to farm the rest of their landlord's fields, and provide various services, such as free transport and work on roads.

Clearly such a system was open to abuse. While the old Tibet was certainly not "the darkest feudal serfdom in the world" as the Chinese were to claim, neither was it the "Shangri-La" of its supporters.

As a young man, the Dalai Lama was acutely aware of this, and one of his great hopes was to change the landowning system to make it fairer. Unfortunately events were to overtake him before he could carry this out.

However, despite Tibet's size, despite the divisions of wealth and status, there was one thing that united peasant, nomad, monk and noble – the Buddhist religion and its embodiment in the person of the Dalai Lama.

Above: A noble family travels in some style across the rugged landscape of Tibet. Despite the religion and culture which united them, there was a wide disparity of wealth and privilege between noble, peasant and nomad.

Opposite: The monastery of Yamdrok Tso clings precariously to the mountainside at five thousand metres above sea level. Before 1950, there were over three thousand monasteries in Tibet – ranging in size from a single building with a handful of monks, to huge complexes, almost small "towns", which ran into many thousands of inhabitants. Today, most of them, including Yamdrok Tso, are derelict ruins.

Buddhism

Although sharing many similarities, Buddhism differs from other religions in one crucial respect – it makes no mention of God.

It was founded by the Lord Buddha on the northern borders of India in the sixth century BC. Born as Prince Siddhartha, his problem was how to interpret and explain the suffering he saw all around him – old age, poverty, disease and death. After much searching, and several false starts, Siddhartha meditated under the now famous Bodhi Tree at Bodh Gaya and achieved "realization" or "enlightenment".

The basis of his subsequent teachings argued that only by accepting that our existence is bound up

with suffering, and that this suffering is the product of our own will and desires, can we ever escape from the endless cycle of death and rebirth which, he believed, is the lot of all living things. Somehow, he taught, we need to loosen the power of desire within us – to let go of the obsession with "I", "me" and "mine". Only by achieving this, said the Buddha, could we reach "nirvana" or the "death-less" – a relaxed state of being in which there was no desire for anything. In this way people could step off from the eternal, whirling merry-go-round and be free at last from suffering.

For the next thousand years, Buddhism flourished in northern India, and spread to many countries in South East Asia and the Far East. At the peak of its development in India, in the seventh century AD, it was carried to Tibet by a number of learned Indian teachers. And there, where the sky is bluer than anywhere else on earth and the

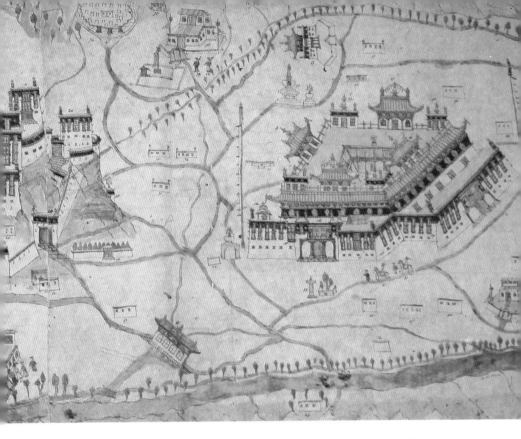

land and mountains more spectacularly barren, the new religion took root.

However, there was one particular aspect of Buddhism that the Tibetans were to emphasize and explore – compassion.

The origins of the Dalai Lamas

About five hundred years after the death of the Lord Buddha, a school, called the "Mahayana", arose that stressed the compassion of Buddhism. Its ideal was that those who had achieved "enlightenment" should return to the earthly realm to teach and help those who were still suffering. It called this sort of person a "Bodhisattva".

It was this version of Buddhism that the Indian teachers were to stress when they came to Tibet. Soon monasteries were established throughout the country, each with its own "reincarnated" abbot

A nineteenth century drawing of Lhasa, showing the Potala (left) – winter palace of the Dalai Lama – and the Johkang temple, the oldest and holiest Buddhist shrine in Tibet. As the place where Buddhism first took root in Tibet, and because of its association with the Dalai Lamas, Lhasa became known as the "Holy City". Pilgrims from all over the country would travel for many months to pray here, some making the entire journey on their knees. When allowed by the Chinese, they still do.

13

who would return again in a new body to carry on the work of his predecessor.

It was in this scheme of things that the first Dalai Lama was born in the fourteenth century. He became the high lama of Drepung Monastery, the largest monastery in Tibet. (In 1950 it housed over seven thousand monks.) From that time, each succeeding Dalai Lama is supposed to be the reincarnation of the previous Dalai Lama. It was the fifth Dalai Lama, who lived in the middle of the seventeenth century, who was to become both spiritual and political leader of all Tibet.

The country was to be ruled by his successors, or their regents, until China's invasion of the 1950s.

The search for the new Dalai Lama

From a western or foreign viewpoint, it is very hard to understand the whole idea of choosing someone as a reincarnation, or rebirth, of a previous person in a new body. Is it possible? And what if you make a mistake? But then there are things in all religions equally as strange, and in the end it comes down to a matter of belief.

There is no doubt that the finding and recognition of the present Dalai Lama is extraordinary – indeed, it sounds rather like a scene from a fairy tale.

As the story goes, the thirteenth Dalai Lama left various signs before he died that he might be reborn in the north-east of Tibet – though these were far from conclusive. After his death in 1933, his body sat in state in the great Potala Palace in traditional Buddhist posture, looking to the south. One morning it was noticed that his head had twisted around overnight to face north-east.

Soon after this, the Regent and a party of high lamas and government officials set out on a pilgrimage to the sacred lake of Lhamo Lhatso. By long tradition it was believed that every person who gazed into its waters would see a part of the future.

After long meditation, the Regent looked into the lake's mirror and reported the following vision. First, the three Tibetan letters – Ah, Ka and Ma – appeared before him. Then the hills of eastern Tibet danced before his eyes. Standing among the hills was a huge monastery with roofs of green and gold, and nearby, along an unused path in a little village, was a simple house with turquoise tiles.

His Holiness is found

Full of excitement, the expedition returned to Lhasa and three search parties set out secretly for the East. (Secrecy was necessary as much of eastern Tibet was under the control of Chinese warlords.) After many days of travel through wild and desolate country in deepest winter, one group reached the very north-east edge of Tibet.

There they observed the green-and-gold roofs of the great monastery of Kumbum glinting in the winter sun. To their great excitement the nearby village of Taktser boasted a house with unmistakable turquoise tiles. The family that lived there had a little boy not quite two years old ...

The search party at once decided to visit the house. However, before going in it was agreed that the leader of the party – the abbot of Sera Monastery – should appear disguised as a servant – the better to observe the boy.

And indeed it was in the servants' quarters that they found the baby of the family. When he saw the Sera Abbot, the boy at once clambered onto his lap and began fingering a rosary the Abbot was wearing around his neck, and asked whether he might have it. The rosary had belonged to the thirteenth Dalai Lama. The Abbot replied that he could have it if he could guess who he was. Without hesitation the child declared that he was a "lama of Sera". The searchers were greatly impressed.

A few days later it was decided to test the boy further. The party wished to find out if the child could remember objects from his past life. A pair of identical black rosaries – one of which had belonged to the thirteenth Dalai Lama – were offered to the boy. Again without hesitation, he chose the one used by the late Dalai Lama. The same test was made with other objects – yellow rosaries, drums and walking sticks – and each time the boy

A unique photograph of the Abbot of Sera monastery taken in 1937. He was one of the leaders of the three search parties that set out eastward to look for the new Dalai Lama. It was while dangling the two-year-old Tenzin Gyatso on his knee that the Abbot's party first realized that they had found their new spiritual leader.

Above: Hundreds of yak butter lamps light up the darkness in the heart of the Johkang temple in the middle of Lhasa. Like the teachings of Buddha, the light is meant to be eternal.

Right: An early hand-painted photograph of a nobleman and his family taken in Lhasa in the 1930s. Such men, together with the heads of the monastic orders, dominated both the civil service and government of the state.

made the correct choice.

Overjoyed, the party decided their search was over. All the signs seen by the Regent in his vision had been fulfilled. Even the Tibetan letters fitted – Ah stood for Amdo; Ka for the monastery of Kumbum; and Ka and Ma together signified the little monastery of Karma Rolpai Dorjee which stood above the village. His Holiness the fourteenth Dalai Lama had been found.

Arrival in Lhasa

The little Dalai Lama was kept safe at Kumbum monastery, where he spent almost a year. Naturally for a child so young, he missed his family and his playmates, and indeed, the only real companion of his own age was his elder brother Lobsang Samten. The two of them played just like any other Tibetan children would – dice, hide-and-seek, races, and also incessant fighting – for neither realized at the time that the younger was the Dalai Lama. The worst problems they caused their guardians was when they disappeared to hide for hours on end. Then there would be wholesale panic while Incarnate lamas and respected elderly monks rushed about trying to find the two children – who thought it all tremendous fun!

At last in 1939, just after his fourth birthday, the Dalai Lama and his party began the long journey to the capital, Lhasa. Most of the party rode or walked, but the Dalai Lama and his brother went in a *treljam* – a sort of sedan-chair carried between two mules. The journey took months as there were no proper roads, but finally they arrived in Lhasa, where in March 1940 the new Dalai Lama, Tenzin Gyatso, was enthroned in the Potala Palace.

H.E. Richardson, a British resident in Tibet, who observed the splendid scenes, later wrote, "The child, not yet five, won the immediate devotion of his people by the incomparable self-possession and charm of his behaviour." He sat calmly through days of ceremonies, that were elaborate – and indeed interminable.

Nobody attending would have believed that in less than twenty years time, the Dalai Lama and

"Even as a child.... He radiated calm, which is very nearly unheard of in a four-year-old, and those who were there will tell how he sat through long ceremonies which would tax even an adult. They describe him as being at once restful and alert, which is a fair description to this day."

Roger Hicks and Ngakpa Chogyam, from their biography, "Great Ocean".

many of his people would be tragically forced to flee their broken country.

A lonely childhood

Perhaps the most poignant descriptions of the Dalai Lama's childhood concern his telescope. Perched on the high roofs of the Potala Palace he would spend hours and hours watching the bustling life of the streets of Lhasa below. The aura surrounding his position meant it was impossible to mix directly with his people, although he was desperately anxious to be part of them. This early experience has almost certainly resulted in the direct and open way that he now leads the Tibetans in exile. Being distanced from his people is one aspect of the old Tibet he would never like to see return.

Although his family had accompanied him to Lhasa, most of his time was spent with tutors or on his own. When not engaged in intensive religious studies, he would wander through the endless rooms of the Potala – each one a treasure trove of the most incredible riches.

He enjoyed taking to pieces and putting together again the antique mechanical toys he found there (presents from the Tsars of Russia in the eighteenth century). He developed an intense interest in all things mechanical which lasts till this day.

News of the outside world

As he grew older Tenzin Gyatso, the young Dalai Lama, did mix with more people. One of his most interesting and rewarding friendships was with Heinrich Harrer, author of *Seven Years in Tibet*. Harrer, an Austrian, had escaped from a British prison camp in India during World War II and walked to Lhasa. He was the first outsider to report back to the West on the "Forbidden Land". For the Tibetans he was the first adventurer to be allowed to influence their unchanged ancient culture.

Harrer met the Dalai Lama when he was a thirteen-year-old, ravenous for news of the outside world. Harrer was soon teaching him English and geography, helping him dismantle a projector and making movie films of life in Lhasa.

Harrer admits to being continually astonished by the quickness and breadth of his intellect – not to mention his mechanical ability which often sent him skipping out to repair the ramshackle palace generator every time it broke down.

But of course, Tenzin Gyatso's main occupation during his early years was studying the immense recital of Buddhist teachings. These studies were academic, in the sense that the West understands the word, but also consisted of regular sessions in meditation and developing the skills of debating on religious subjects. The Dalai Lama excelled. Heinrich Harrer witnessed the fourteen-year-old's first public debate with the Abbot of Drepung and wrote, "It was a genuine contest of wits in which the Abbot was hard put to it to hold his own."

However, even as he was debating, forces were massing outside Tibet that were soon to change its

Above: In a timeless scene, young monks debate points of theology from the Buddhist scriptures in a courtyard of the massive Drepung Monastery outside Lhasa. Study and debate were essential parts of the Dalai Lama's education.

Opposite above: Studying the holy texts – a large part of any monk's day.

Opposite below: His Holiness displays a shy smile in one of the earliest pictures taken of him.

A nomad woman. Almost
half the population of
Tibet lived as wandering
nomads tending their
herds of yaks and ponies.
It was a hard life, ranging
across the high pastures of
some of the most rugged
terrain in the world, but
the people were peaceful
and happy.

nature and the life of the Dalai Lama forever. In
1949, the communists won the civil war in China.
"The task for the People's Liberation Army for
1950," declared Radio Peking in its New Year broadcast, "is to liberate Tibet."

Tibet and China

For centuries an uneasy relationship had existed
between Tibet and China. In the seventh to ninth
centuries AD, Tibet had been a strong military
power whose influence reached to the gates of
China's capital, Peking, itself. By the time of the
first Dalai Lamas, however, China had become the
stronger, though she never attempted to rule Tibet
in any more than name.

Indeed, during this time a special relationship
developed between the two peoples. The Mongol
Emperors of China had first been converted to
Buddhism by the Tibetans and looked to them for
guidance in religious matters. In return, the Mongol
Emperors offered to protect and support Tibet in
more worldly affairs.

Political turbulence in Tibet at the beginning of
the eighteenth century gave the new Chinese
Manchu dynasty a chance to extend its influence
to a limited extent. Two permanent Chinese
ambassadors were stationed in Lhasa, supposedly
to enforce the Emperor's will. In practice, however,
Lhasa was too far away and too remote for the
Chinese to influence very much. So, apart from a
few brief flurries of military activity, the Tibetans
were left to get on with ruling themselves as they
always had done.

The last flurry took place in 1910, when Tibet
was brutally invaded by a particularly vicious
Chinese warlord. He had misjudged his timing,
however. In 1911 revolution swept across China,
carrying away the old order and the emperors with
it. The Tibetans seized their chance. All the Chinese
were thrown out of Tibet and total independence
was declared against a country which it was felt,
by its invasion, had forfeited any right to a special
relationship.

The argument about whether Tibet was an independent state rages to this day with lawyers from both sides digging up learned reasons from the mists of history. However, it is worth quoting a report drawn up by the International Commission of Jurists – a distinguished body of impartial experts – which was submitted to the United Nations in 1959:

"Tibet's position on the expulsion of the Chinese in 1912 can fairly be described as one of *de facto* independence and there are strong legal grounds for thinking that any form of legal subservience to China had vanished. It is therefore submitted that the events of 1911-1912 mark the re-emergence of Tibet as a fully sovereign state, independent in fact and in law of Chinese control."

However, it remained the case that when China threatened Tibet in 1950, the rest of the world knew virtually nothing whatever about the country and its position in regard to powerful China.

As the Dalai Lama was to lament in exile, "If only we had applied to join the League of Nations or the United Nations, or even appointed ambassadors to a few of the leading powers, I am sure these signs of sovereignty would have been accepted without question." As it was, the Tibetan government, ruling on behalf of the young Dalai Lama, did not act until Tibet's danger was acute, and then what they did was too little and too late.

A Tibet peasant. The staple crop of the peasant was barley which thrives at high altitude. Later, when the Chinese arrived in 1950, they forced the farmers to grow wheat instead – with disastrous results.

Desperate actions

By the summer of 1949, this time had come. The Tibetan government's first action was to expel the entire Chinese delegation, for fear it was already sheltering Chinese agitators. A Tibetan band escorted them courteously, but firmly, out of Lhasa and on the road to India. The government then feverishly set to work to reorganize and increase the size of the army. Training camps were established in the fields around Lhasa, new regiments were recruited, and even a National Anthem was composed – to replace the British "God Save the King" which had served up till now.

As a noisy propaganda campaign from Radio

The mask of an evil spirit. Before the Buddhist religion reached Tibet, people believed in a spirit world and many of these beliefs became interwoven with the new religion. In times of trouble, omens and devils became a potent force.

"When the Chinese first came in 1950, they gave the farmers tools and said they had come to help us. But four years later they had taken control of everything themselves ... and pushed the Tibetans to the outskirts. My family is an example – two jumped in the water and committed suicide; one died in prison; one hanged himself. All my lands were taken away. These events should never happen to any human being."

A Tibetan farmer, interviewed secretly for British television.

Peking was stepped up, the Tibetan government started broadcasting its own views of the situation through two British radio operators who were in Tibet at this time. (Together they made up a third of the "massive" number of Anglo-American "imperialists" whom Radio Peking claimed were running Tibet. In fact there were only six westerners in Tibet in 1950.) Delegations were also appointed to visit Peking, Delhi, Washington and London. Unfortunately, they never got further than India, as they were refused audiences. Meanwhile, the Chinese assured the world that there was no need for foreign interference in an "internal matter".

As well as taking these practical steps to defend Tibet, the government also appealed to the spiritual forces of the people. Religion was the most powerful element in Tibetan society, and in their hour of danger, the Tibetans called upon it to save them. All the monks in Tibet attended public services: new prayer wheels were set up and incense burned from the mountain tops day and night.

Heinrich Harrer has written touchingly about the zeal and enthusiasm that went into the religious festivals of early 1950. "They surpassed in pomp and splendour anything I had ever seen," he wrote. "It seemed as if the whole population of Tibet had gathered, in pious enthusiasm, in the narrow streets of Lhasa."

Despite everything, the faith of the Tibetan people remained unshakeable. Those days were like the last bright flame of a candle that was soon to be snuffed out forever.

Ill omens

Yet the news from the East continued to be bad. Tibet's National Assembly now sat in almost continual session. The State Oracle was frequently consulted, but all the prophecies were of doom and disaster and did nothing to cheer up the people. Nor were they cheered by a spate of disasters that occurred during Tibet's last summer of independence. The Tibetan people believed in omens and none of the signs were good. On August 15, 1950 a massive earthquake in eastern Tibet buried hundreds of monks and nuns in the rubble of their monasteries, and caused panic in Lhasa.

After this, wrote Heinrich Harrer, "the evil omens multiplied. Monsters were born. One morning the capital of the stone column at the foot of the Potala was found lying on the ground in fragments ... and when one day in blazing summer weather water began to flow from a gargoyle on the cathedral, the people of Lhasa were beside themselves with terror."

On the eastern frontier the poorly-equipped and under-trained Tibetan troops waited nervously for the Chinese, who were already infiltrating the border areas. But as summer ended and the first winter storms began to blow, they started to relax a little.

Robert Ford, a British radio operator based in the area at the time, recalls talking to the governor of the province at the beginning of October. "The Chinese cannot hope to reach Lhasa this year," said the governor, "they will not try before the spring." Robert Ford agreed with him.

A week later the Chinese invaded.

A noble lady from a powerful family in all the finery of her traditional costume. All such dress was banned after 1959.

Invasion

As dawn broke on October 7, 1950, overwhelming numbers of Chinese cavalry and infantry launched a massive, simultaneous attack on the heartland of Tibet from six different places. Doggedly the tiny Tibetan army tried to halt the invaders at river crossings and mountain passes, but there was no stopping the Chinese tide. In a matter of weeks, the Tibetan forces had been split up and surrounded, and the Chinese People's Liberation Army had advanced many miles into Tibet.

News of the attack took ten days to reach Lhasa. When the first stories arrived they caused great concern. For months now, popular opinion had been urging that the Dalai Lama himself should take power in place of the indecisive Regent and his helpers. With the news of the disasters at the frontier, this feeling became a demand.

And so, at the age of barely fifteen, the fourteenth Dalai Lama took on the enormous responsibility of directing his country at the most desperate moment of its entire history. (Despite the situation, great celebrations were held at the installation – the Tibetan's love of parties is a by-word!)

Soldiers train in the Lhasa valley as fear of invasion mounts. Ill-equipped, ill-trained and ill-armed, the Tibetan army, despite its dogged resistance, stood no chance against the Communist People's Liberation Army. The army had never been allowed to grow strong in Tibet, partly because it was seen as a threat to the power of the monks, particularly the powerful monasteries around Lhasa, and partly because Tibetans relied on the inhospitable nature of their country's terrain to defend them.

An appeal to the rest of the world

The first action of the Dalai Lama and his new ministers was to send an urgent appeal to the United Nations for help. "As long as the people of Tibet are compelled by force to become a part of China against their will and consent," declared the appeal, "the present invasion of Tibet will be the grossest instance of the violation of the weak by the strong."

The Tibetans, in their innocence, put great faith in the justice of the United Nations. Unfortunately, as we have seen, Tibet was not a member, and the rest of the world knew almost nothing about the country. The result was a deafening silence, and the question of Tibet was not raised again on an international level for a further nine years. Thus abandoned, the Tibetans were left to defend themselves as best they could.

Fight on – or talk?

The failure of this appeal was a bitter blow to the Dalai Lama. By now Chinese forces had advanced deep into eastern Tibet, and were calling upon the government to surrender. Greatly alarmed, the cabinet and the National Assembly urged Tenzin Gyatso to leave Lhasa at once and go to Yatung on the Indian border. There he would be able to escape to plead his country's cause if necessary.

With great reluctance, for he did not wish to abandon his people, His Holiness agreed to the move. In the cold dawn of a December morning, it was a sad and dispirited column that escorted the fifteen-year-old Tibetan ruler out of Lhasa, where he had reigned for only a few weeks, and onto the road to the border.

At Yatung, the Dalai Lama went over the situation again and again in his mind. In the end he decided that it would be best, if possible, to try to placate the Chinese and live peacefully with them.

He did this principally to avoid further bloodshed and misery on both sides. But it should also be remembered that the Dalai Lama has never opposed communism in theory. As he was later to say in exile, "The aims of the Lord Buddha and of Karl

A Tibetan stamp showing the stylized snowlion in the middle – the symbol of Tibet.

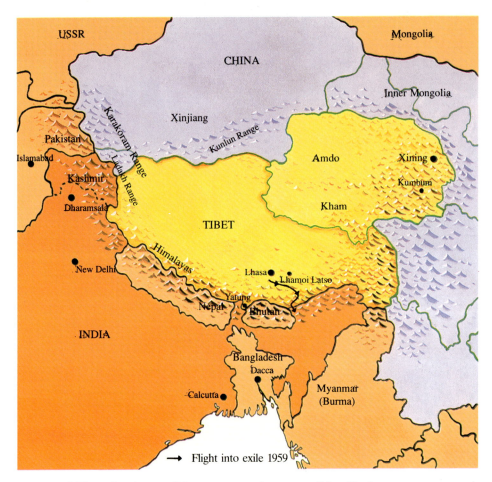

USSR

CHINA

Mongolia

Inner Mongolia

Xinjiang

Karakoram Range

Kunlun Range

Pakistan

Islamabad

Amdo

Xining

Kashmir

Ladakh Range

Kumbum

Dharamsala

Kham

TIBET

Himalayas

New Delhi

Lhasa

Lhamoi Latso

Yatung

Nepal

Bhutan

INDIA

Bangladesh

Dacca

Myanmar
(Burma)

Calcutta

→ Flight into exile 1959

A map of Tibet showing the present autonomous region and the eastern provinces of Amdo and Kham (now part of Chinese provinces). Also shown is the path of the Dalai Lama's flight to India and his present residence in Dharamsala.

Marx are not incompatible. Both were concerned with bringing happiness to the masses, the Buddha with spiritual happiness and Marx with material happiness. Is it not reasonable, then, to see how the two might work together?"

As a consequence of these deliberations, a peace delegation was sent to the Chinese.

The Chinese promises

Negotiations between the two sides took place in Peking, and ended in the signing on May 23, 1951 of what has become known as the Seventeen Point Agreement. This was the first treaty signed between Tibet and China since 821 AD, and it was clear that the Tibetan delegates had no choice but to agree to everything put in front of them. The delegation was not allowed even to consult the Dalai Lama or the Tibetan government for instructions. Furthermore they were threatened with massive military action against Tibet if the delegates refused to sign. The Chinese even went to the lengths of forging duplicate seals of the Tibetan government to affix on the dictated documents.

Tibet was declared an integral part of China, and henceforth her foreign affairs, defence and communications would be run by Peking. In return, the Chinese made promises to make no change in the political system of Tibet or the position of the Dalai Lama, and to respect the religion and customs of the Tibetan people. The lama monasteries would be protected. In the meantime, large Chinese forces would occupy Tibet to see that the Agreement was carried out.

Accordingly, in September 1951 the Chinese General, Chang Chin-wu, arrived in Lhasa with three thousand picked troops. Twenty thousand more were sent to other key places in Tibet. Deeply saddened by these events, the Dalai Lama nonetheless agreed to return to try to work with the Chinese, in the hope that his presence might soften the blow that had so tragically befallen his people.

Thus without any choice and abandoned by an ignorant world, Tibet as an independent nation ceased to exist.

The Chinese troops arrive

When Tenzin Gyatso returned to Lhasa at the end of 1951, he found resentment against the Chinese already growing. More troops continued to flow into the capital and houses were taken over by Chinese officers and officials. A huge army camp was set up in the pleasant meadows by the river – a beautiful picnic spot for the Lhasa people in happier times.

But worst of all, the Chinese troops had brought no food with them. They began by demanding the delivery of two thousand tons of barley from the Tibetan people. This was soon followed by a further demand, then another, and another.... For the first time in living memory, the fear of famine haunted the streets of Lhasa.

What was the attitude of the Dalai Lama as he watched the anger of his people growing against the invaders of their land? In his book *My Land and My People*, His Holiness spells out the practical and moral reasons why he adopted the difficult path of conciliation with the uninvited guests that now occupied his country.

To begin with, it was clear that the Tibetans did not have the means to oppose the Chinese by force – to try to do so would invite destruction. "Our only hope," wrote His Holiness, "was to persuade the Chinese peaceably to fulfil the promises they had made in their agreement. Non-violence was the only course which might win us back a degree of freedom in the end, perhaps after years of patience." The moral reasons for rejecting violence were even more powerful – "Non-violence was the only moral course," His Holiness argued. "This was not only my own profound belief, it was clearly in accordance with the teachings of Lord Buddha, and as the religious leader of Tibet I was bound to uphold it."

Thus in the early 1950s, the young Tibetan leader who had been thrust so abruptly into the thick of Tibet's political nightmare, attempted to follow the near-impossible task of balancing increasing Chinese demands with the growing resentment of his people.

"Tibet is a distinct and ancient nation, which for many centuries enjoyed a relationship of mutual respect with China. It is true that there were times when China was strong and Tibet was weak, and China invaded Tibet. Similarly, looking farther back into history, there were times when Tibet invaded China. There is no basis whatever in history for the Chinese claim that Tibet was part of China."

The Dalai Lama, from "My Land and My People".

The tragedy begins to unfold

We might also ask what the Chinese attitude to the Tibetans was in the years following the invasion. The reasons why the communist leaders were determined to "liberate" Tibet were probably a mixture of the idealogical and the practical. One of Mao Tse-tung's ideals was to add Tibet to the "big family" of the People's Republic of China, and to free its inhabitants from what he regarded as "feudal tyranny".

The Chinese may perhaps be forgiven for not

understanding the strong independent feeling of the Tibetans. Certainly, Tibetan society was not perfect. Many peasants and nomads were very poor, and the landowning system was unfair – as has been mentioned. But it does seem that most Tibetans, from whatever background, were united in supporting their traditional way of life – particularly the religious traditions that bound them all together. There has never been a peasant uprising in Tibet, which contrasts strongly with the many revolts that have taken place in China. This cultural misunderstanding was to be a major contribution to the tragedy that was about to unfold.

Of course the Chinese had highly practical reasons for wishing to swallow Tibet. The possibility of finding precious minerals was a rich spur. But more importantly was the key position Tibet occupied in central Asia. This position the Chinese, with their nuclear weapons, still exploit to this day.

But the Chinese were also down to earth in their dealings with the Tibetans during these early years of occupation. They realized they could not impose sweeping changes at once. Instead they intended to use the old form of government – and particularly

A rare, early photograph of a group of Ralpa – wandering entertainers who, in happier times, journeyed from village to village delighting people with their dance, mime and songs.

the person of the Dalai Lama – as the means by which they could gradually extend their influence.

Thus, once in Lhasa, the Chinese commanders did not dismiss the nobility and monks from their positions as government officials. Nor did they attempt to introduce the peasants to the ideas of communism. Instead they began by setting them to work building roads – for this was the practical way in which China would dominate Tibet – and concentrated on winning over the ruling classes. For a few years, then, things would continue roughly as before – in the main area of Tibet at least.

On the borders it was tragically different ...

Visit to Peking

Although outwardly respecting the position of the Dalai Lama, almost at once the Chinese began chipping away at the Tibetans' freedom to control their affairs. In 1952, they demanded the dismissal of the Dalai Lama's two prime ministers, and insisted that in future no appointment should be made without their consent. Nor would they allow the Dalai Lama to start introducing his own reforms of the landowning system, which he had begun preparing almost as soon as he returned to Lhasa. Propaganda attacks began on the monasteries and their position in Tibetan society.

All this caused mounting tension in the capital, but, as yet, there were no open clashes. And indeed, in 1954, the Dalai Lama agreed to go to Peking to meet the communist leaders.

When the Dalai Lama and the Chinese-educated Panchen Lama (the second highest lama in Tibet) arrived in Peking they were greeted by regimented, cheering crowds. His Holiness confessed later that he had the uncomfortable feeling that they would as readily have been jeering and hissing if that was what they had been told to do.

His Holiness had a number of meetings with Mao Tse-tung, and the two leaders seemed to get on quite well together. The Tibetans had to endure many flowery speeches (some seven hours long) describing the "great progress" that had been made

in Tibet since the invasion. After five months the twenty-year-old Tenzin Gyatso and his party left China with what they hoped was a firm promise that real self government would be granted to Tibet.

However, His Holiness's feelings of guarded optimism were not to survive the long journey home through the suffering border areas of eastern Tibet. Here he found that resentment against the Chinese humiliations was at boiling point, and had been since the invasion began four years before.

The Dalai Lama is welcomed by the Chinese on his visit to Peking in 1954. Initial optimism that the Communists would keep their promises did not outlast the visit, however. From left to right: Chu Teh, Vice-Chairman of the Central People's Government, the Dalai Lama, the Panchen Lama and Premier Chou En-lai.

Oppression

In the border provinces of Amdo and Kham – areas long semi-independent from the central governments of both China and Tibet – the Chinese had decided to introduce sweeping reforms almost at once. This was a grave mistake, for these provinces contained a Tibetan population just like anywhere else in the country – a Tibetan population, moreover, which was more independently minded and arguably more devoutly religious than any other.

Andrug Gombo Tashi, later to become the hero of the Tibetan revolt, described what happened in his memoirs: "In my area of Kham, the local population was divided into five groups (according to wealth or position) and a terror campaign of selective arrests was launched by the Chinese. People belonging to the first three groups were either publicly humiliated or condemned to the firing squad. The Chinese destroyed thousands of monasteries, lamas and monks were imprisoned without reason, while others were subjected to various humiliations or condemned to death."

By 1954 the Chinese were introducing new forms of taxation, land reforms, and inflicting severe punishments on ordinary people who continued to follow their religion.

The first guerrillas

At the same time they tried to disarm the people of Kham province. To the ordinary Kham peasant, his sword or rifle was considered as much a part of his body as his arm or his leg. He was not going to let anyone deprive him of his independence without resisting. Nor was he going to remain unmoved while his religion was attacked. People took to the hills in droves and soon guerrilla bands were springing up all over eastern Tibet.

By 1956 so many Tibetans were fighting that the Chinese were forced to launch a huge military operation against them. Planes and tanks were moved in and pockets of resistance such as the monasteries of Lithang and Batang were completely destroyed. Savage punishments were meted out to villagers thought to be aiding the guerrillas, and large numbers of Chinese were brought in to take over their lands. Faced with the might of the Chinese army, the guerrilla tribesmen began moving westward to central Tibet and Lhasa – bringing revolt with them.

Soon after the Dalai Lama's return from China, it became increasingly obvious that Mao Tse-tung's promise of self-government for Tibet meant very little in practice. The "Unified Preparatory Committee for the Autonomous Region of Tibet", which was set up to achieve this, was packed with Chinese supporters and simply said yes to everything Peking demanded.

In the capital, Lhasa, things were not going well. Resistance to the Chinese was growing. Posters denouncing the Chinese and their interference with the Dalai Lama's powers and the traditions of Tibet began to appear on the city's walls. As whispers of the uprisings in the East started to reach the capital popular leaders emerged to denounce the Chinese. They were immediately arrested.

Cairns of "prayer stones" like this exist all over Tibet on mountain tops, river sides and valley bottoms. Each stone is carved and white-washed to emphasize the prayers carved on them by the Buddhist believers. The Chinese pulled down the monasteries but they could not destroy the simple faith of the ordinary people.

Journey to India

Despite the grim goings on in Tibet, 1956 was also the date of a much happier event – the 2,500th anniversary of the enlightenment of the Lord Buddha. The Dalai Lama, now aged twenty-one, was personally invited to the ceremonies by the government of India. Although greatly put out, the Chinese could not refuse him permission to go.

Later, His Holiness was to say that arriving in India was almost like coming home than going to a foreign country – so overwhelming was his welcome by the Indian government and the Indian people. On his arrival in Delhi he made a speech at the Rajghat, where Mahatma Gandhi – Indian leader and champion of the doctrine of non-violence – was cremated. Not surprisingly, his

A guerrilla's gau or amulet containing a picture of the young Dalai Lama. The Tibetans wear them in reverence and for protection. For example, when one guerrilla leader was asked why he ran straight into enemy fire he replied, "How could they kill me? I had the Dalai Lama's gau so the bullets must go by."

theme was peace, and he was to affirm here something that he has said again many times since: the salvation of humanity lies in the "religious" (in its broadest sense) instinct that lies in all of us. And it is the forcible repression of this instinct by the individual or by society that is the enemy of peace.

As he continued his pilgrimage to Bodh Gaya he was to preach this message to the thousands of people – Buddhists, Hindus, Muslims, Christians – who waited to greet him and seek his blessing.

The Dalai Lama also used this opportunity to make political contacts whenever possible. He met the Indian Prime Minister, Nehru, who was sympathetic but not inclined to interfere with the affairs of the more powerful China. He also talked to the Chinese Prime Minister, Chou-En lai, who happened to be in India at the time. Chou apologized for the "over-zealous actions" of some Chinese officials. He repeated Mao's promise in Peking that Tibet should have real independence as soon as the Tibetans could manage their own affairs. This was a curious offer, because they had been doing so perfectly well before the Chinese arrived – nonetheless it was of some comfort to the Dalai Lama.

The Dalai Lama as a young man. It must be remembered that throughout this disastrous time His Holiness was not yet twenty-four.

Breaking point

His return to Lhasa was to dispel such comfort.

Horrific stories of the rape, torture and execution of Tibetan communities by the Chinese occupying army were pouring in from the East. Villages and monasteries were being bombed and shelled on the mere suspicion of aiding guerrillas. And resistance was growing.

To Tenzin Gyatso it was clear that the Chinese had by now given up all attempts to impose their will other than by force. All hopes of even semi-independence had gone out of the door. Uprisings continued to break out in the East throughout 1957, and by the end of that year they were beginning to be co-ordinated nationally. Led by Andrug Gombo Tashi, a national guerrilla movement calling itself *Chushi Gangdrug,* meaning "Four Rivers, Six Ranges", was soon operating all over Tibet.

By the summer of 1958, the guerrilla leader was conducting lightning raids nearer and nearer the capital. Within a few months, he had grown so bold that he was able to wipe out a Chinese garrison a mere twenty-five miles from Lhasa. The result was to raise anti-Chinese feelings in the capital to fever pitch. Local resistance groups left to join the guerrillas. Even some important government officials gave them encouragement – though to this day the guerrillas claim that they were let down by lack of support from the government in Lhasa.

The rising anger of his people left the Dalai Lama in a terrible position. He was totally against violence

The Potala – the winter palace of the Dalai Lamas. Dominating Lhasa's skyline, and indeed the country for miles around, the magnificent red, white and gold of the palace seem to epitomize all the mysteries of Tibet. A castle had existed here since the seventh century A.D., but the present building with its endless corridors and shrines and priceless treasures was begun in the seventeenth century by the Fifth Dalai Lama. It only narrowly escaped destruction by the Chinese during the Cultural Revolution because of the personal intervention of Chou En-lai.

of any kind, yet he found it hard to condemn the simple tribesmen who had been provoked to breaking point and were now sacrificing their lives in his name. To the end he tried to calm his angry people, but ultimately this proved beyond even his powers.

Meanwhile, despite the chaos taking place all around him, Tenzin Gyatso still found time to study and sit for his *Geshé* degree – the highest academic degree in Tibet. To pass the examination, he had to face thirty of the most learned lamas in open debate for a whole day. The fact that he was awarded the degree when he was barely twenty-four – most lamas attempted it when in their thirties or forties

– is remarkable. The fact that he achieved this at a time when the whole country was in ferment is even more so – though it is true that at the end of 1958 Lhasa was about the only place in Tibet that retained some semblance of normality.

However, as the new year turned, tension was stretched to breaking point here, too. It just needed a spark for Lhasa to explode.

In March 1959 that explosion came.

Lhasa erupts

As evening fell over Lhasa on March 9, 1959, the city seethed with anger and resentment. On street corners and in crowded cafés and houses, the same question was asked – "How can we stop His Holiness from visiting the Chinese camp tomorrow?"

For over the previous few days the suspicions of the Tibetans had been aroused. During an important ceremony in the temple, the Dalai Lama had been repeatedly interrupted by Chinese officials demanding that he give a date when he could attend a theatrical performance at the Chinese army camp. A few days later he was told that he was to come without his usual bodyguard, or many of his trusted officials. To the people of Lhasa this invitation sounded suspiciously like a trap to kidnap their beloved leader (something not without precedence in Tibetan history).

So before anyone settled down to sleep on that fateful night in early March, the people began to arm themselves with any ancient weapon that came to hand. For nearly eight years, the capital had borne Chinese domination, but they were not going to allow the invaders to steal their Dalai Lama – the very symbol of Tibet itself.

Today, people are still unsure about what the Chinese really meant to do on that ominous day. Certainly their actions were suspicious. It is true that they did wish the Dalai Lama to go to Peking to attend the Chinese National Assembly in the following month – something he was not keen to do. Whether they were prepared to kidnap him to achieve this, however, is another matter.

But what is important is that the people of Lhasa sincerely believed the Dalai Lama was in danger, and this is why they acted as they did.

Thirty thousand on guard

Before dawn on the morning of March 10, thousands of Tibetans were streaming out of Lhasa to the Norbulingka – the Summer Palace – where the Dalai Lama was staying. By midday, over thirty thousand people surrounded the residence. Most were to remain there for the next ten days.

On March 10, 1959 Lhasa's citizens prepared to protect their Dalai Lama from what they feared was a Chinese plot to kidnap him. Thousands were killed when the Communists brutally suppressed this demonstration. March 10 is remembered with anger, pride and tears as the day of the "Tibetan Uprising".

Tibetan refugees seek asylum at the Indian border following the suppression of the uprising in Lhasa. Despite having to dodge Chinese border patrols, around eight thousand followed the Dalai Lama into exile. Most were destitute and many had lost their families.

The mood of the crowd was ugly, and angrily anti-Chinese. Slogans demanding the expulsion of the invaders and freedom for Tibet were chanted. And when a Tibetan official wearing Chinese dress tried to enter the palace, he was stoned to death. Soon units of the Tibetan army – after hurriedly discarding their Chinese uniforms – also joined the crowd. All were united in their desire to protect the Dalai Lama and prevent him from falling into Chinese hands.

His Holiness, meanwhile, was deeply distressed. His one thought was to prevent a massacre of his people. He feared, rightly, that this is what would happen if the protest was prolonged. Thus he continued to negotiate with the Chinese – at the same time trying to persuade the people to return home.

But the crowd stubbornly refused to disperse. They were not going to submit meekly to Chinese rule again without a fight.

As the days went by, ominous movements could be seen taking place in and around the Chinese camp. More troops appeared and heavy guns were positioned on hills surrounding the Norbulingka. On March 17, two mortar shells were fired into the grounds of the palace. The Dalai Lama and his advisers took this for a sign that all their attempts to prevent an open break with the Chinese had failed. The communists, it appeared, were now prepared to slaughter the protesters – even if this meant killing the Dalai Lama as well.

With a heavy heart, for he did not wish to abandon his people, His Holiness made the momentous decision to escape. If Tibet was to be destroyed, at least her living symbol – the Dalai Lama – should survive to carry the torch.

Escape

As night fell, Tenzin Gyatso, with his family and close advisers, prepared to leave. After praying for the last time in the peace of his chapel, His Holiness changed into the simple clothing of a common soldier. With a rifle slung over his shoulder, he and his small party slipped unnoticed out of the

Norbulingka and into the darkness.

The first few miles were fraught with danger, for the fugitives had to pass very close to the Chinese camp. However, they succeeded in passing unnoticed, and soon met up with a group of Khampa guerrillas who were waiting to escort them. Wasting no time, the whole party headed for the wilderness of southern Tibet.

The following days were ones of ceaseless riding through sheer valleys and across dizzy passes – a time of discomfort, cold and great sorrow.

Ill and weary, the Dalai Lama and his small escort cross the Zsagola Pass in the wilds of southern Tibet. The horrific news from Lhasa of the massacre of his people meant there was no option for him but to go on to India – and exile.

The Norbulingka massacre

After journeying for about a week, the terrible news reached the Dalai Lama that the Norbulingka had been bombarded, the crowds massacred and his government dissolved by the Chinese. Up until this point, His Holiness had hoped to set up the government near the border, but now the Chinese would hunt him out wherever he went. The only course was to cross into India.

This rare photograph shows monks surrendering from Sera monastery, Lhasa, following the suppression of the March 10 uprising. Chinese propaganda newsreel made much of these scenes, for viewing in China, to label the Tibetans as backward and ignorant reactionaries from a feudal age.

And so on March 31, 1959 ill, weary and more unhappy than he has ever been able to express, the Dalai Lama left his country for exile.

Two days after the Dalai Lama's flight from the Norbulingka, and without knowing whether he was there or not (they looked for him among the bodies later), the Chinese opened fire. The Tibetans stood no chance against the communists' superior weapons, and soon the grounds around the palace and the streets of Lhasa were strewn with bodies.

In the following days, the uprising was savagely suppressed and its leaders executed. A reign of terror was to envelop Tibet.

Reign of terror

Before 1950, the Tibetan people followed a unique religion, culture and way of life – that worked. It was not perfect, but it could claim to be, perhaps, the last great ancient civilization left in the world.

Following the brutal suppression of the uprising in Lhasa, the Chinese swiftly set about trying to destroy everything that, over the centuries, had made Tibet so uniquely different.

From April 1959, any pretext of allowing the Tibetans any say in conducting their own affairs was abandoned. A virtual military dictatorship was set up in Lhasa – though a few Tibetans willing to co-operate remained in the government. Sweeping reforms were now immediately introduced throughout Tibet. A reign of terror was begun against all those thought to have aided or even sympathized with the recent uprising.

Genocide

Nobles and landowners were imprisoned, humiliated and often shot. High lamas and monks came in for special persecution. Monasteries were emptied, the buildings destroyed, and the monks then forced to do the most degrading tasks.

Dawa Norbu, author of *Red Star Over Tibet*, has described the reactions of ordinary people when this happened in his village of Sakya: "When we saw our most venerated lamas, who were our "gods" just a few days before, carrying human excrement, mixing it with water and sprinkling it all over a newly made Chinese vegetable garden, many shed tears."

Worse was to happen to thousands of others – death by starvation in work camps or execution in horrifying ways. Nor did the poorest peasants escape from this wave of persecution. Anyone even suspected of opposing Chinese rule was punished and executed. So bad was the situation at this time that a Commission of the United Nations – on the evidence of the thousands of Tibetan refugees pouring into India – described the Chinese treatment of the Tibetan people as "genocide".

"The Chinese People's Liberation Army surrounded the great monastery and evicted its 4000 monks. Some of the incarnate lamas and abbots committed suicide, some were later shot; all the rest were deported to labour camps. The Panchen Lama was appalled. Two years later, with tremendous courage, he publicly denounced the Chinese occupation of Tibet and declared his support for the Dalai Lama. He was 'tried', assaulted and was last seen being driven out of Lhasa, with his parents and close followers, in a Chinese Army truck."
Simon Normanton, from "Tibet. The Lost Civilization".

"It is therefore the considered view of the International Commission of Jurists that the evidence points to:
a) a prima-facie case of genocide contrary to Article 2(a) and (e) of the Genocide Convention of 1948:
b) A prima-facie case of a systematic intention by such acts to destroy in whole or in part the Tibetans as a separate nation and the Buddhist religion in Tibet."
From the report of the International Commission of Jurists, 1959.

Living under the communist system

A complete reorganization or "collectivization" of agriculture was now extended to the whole country. This meant that individuals no longer owned land, instead groups worked the land together. Collective farms were part of the communist system. They had partly succeeded in China because the peasants had believed in communism. In Tibet, they were a disaster.

The great estates of the nobles and monasteries were broken up and everywhere in Tibet, peasants were divided into groups of about ten families – called Mutual Aid Teams – to work on the land. Unending work and frequent propaganda sessions on the joys of the new communist regime became

Opposite top: Perched on a mountainside thirty kilometres from Lhasa, the giant monastery of Ganden – once home to six thousand monks – was dynamited by Red Guards during the Cultural Revolution. Its destruction was total.

Opposite bottom: A Tibetan "Library". Centuries of learning and wisdom went into producing the holy literature of Tibet. A few months of wanton destruction obliterated most of it.

the lot of everyone. As Dawa Norbu wrote, "By the end of April [1959] our life had acquired a new pattern; it fell into a dull routine from which no one could escape. Meetings and work. Work and meetings."

Nor, as one might perhaps have expected, did the poor peasants gain anything from the redivision of land in Tibet. Indeed, many in the East lost theirs altogether as new colonists from China arrived to take over their farms.

The families on collective farms were kept on a bare minimum diet for years. Huge amounts of food were needed to feed the growing number of Chinese officials that now appeared in the country and also to satisfy the vast number of troops

"The destruction was wholesale and calculated. Every building of religious or historical importance was desecrated; the ruins of some, like the great monastery of Ganden, were dynamited. Books and scriptures that were not burnt were used as lavatory paper. Things of gold, silver or bronze were pulled down and shipped to China for smelting. It was an attempt at the extermination of an entire culture."
Simon Normanton, from "Tibet. The Lost Civilization".

stationed in Tibet. Troop numbers were increased even further when war broke out between China and India in 1962, and have remained at over a quarter of a million ever since.

The compulsory conversion from the Tibetans' traditional crop of barley, which does well at high altitudes, to wheat, which doesn't, was a disaster. The change was made chiefly to satisfy the tastes of the Chinese occupiers, but it had very damaging effects on the soil and caused widespread famine. The years 1959-1962 were particularly bad and hundreds of thousands are thought to have died. But there were outbreaks of famine throughout the 1960s and 1970s.

The Cultural Revolution

In the years following 1959, Tibetan culture and traditions continued to be attacked and destroyed. All education – such as there was – was now taught in Chinese. Religion was declared to be "poison" and effectively banned. Many young children were

A blatantly-posed Chinese propaganda picture depicts a Tibetan in "traditional costume" trying to operate modern technology. In reality very little of this machinery ever reached the Tibetans. After the Cultural Revolution, even the traditional costume would be banned.

46

forcibly removed from their parents and sent to China to be taught Chinese ideals. Meanwhile Chinese officials continued to run Tibet.

In 1966, the movement called the "Cultural Revolution" was launched in China by the communist leaders. One of the aims of the movement was to destroy everything to do with the past.

In Tibet, it resulted in another wave of destruction against Buddhist shrines and monasteries. Red Guards from the Chinese army invaded Tibet's holiest shrine – the Johkang temple in Lhasa – and smashed all the holy statues and images they could find. The great monastery of Ganden near Lhasa, once the home of over six thousand monks, was reduced to a pile of rubble. Today it looks more like a Roman ruin than a building inhabited by human beings a mere thirty years ago. Perhaps most heartbreaking of all, 60% of all Tibet's sacred literature was deliberately burned.

More arrests and imprisonments accompanied these acts of vandalism.

The rape of the land

Meanwhile, the communists were exploiting Tibet's natural resources as hard as they could. The Chinese call Tibet "the western treasure house" – with good reason. For the country is rich in a wide variety of largely untapped minerals, including uranium, oil, coal, copper and gold.

The province of Kham is, or was, heavily forested. Today these forests are devastated and there are no signs of a replanting policy. Over the last thirty years, China has earned itself fifty-four million dollars from the export of Tibetan timber – and forests are still being felled at the rate of one truck-load a minute.

For years after 1959, small bands of guerrillas continued to attack the Chinese from remote retreats deep in the mountains. But most ordinary Tibetans had little choice but to submit to foreign rule, which, in reality, was a form of colonialism of the harshest kind. Only at the end of the 1970s was there any easing of the situation.

Nomad children from southern Tibet. Chinese rule did not, as they claimed, bring material benefit to the masses. Indeed, by treating the Tibetans as a colonial people, things steadily got worse.

47

In exile

After his perilous journey, the Dalai Lama was greeted with great warmth by the Indian Government and the Indian people and he and his followers were granted asylum.

The Dalai Lama eventually made his headquarters at Dharamsala, a beautiful, old, British hill station that lies at the foot of the first towering rock barrier of the Himalayas.

Tenzin Gyatso's most pressing problem was taking care of the thousands of refugees flooding across the border. And over the next thirty years, groups of persecuted Tibetan refugees continued to cross into India. In all, nearly one hundred thousand have escaped the Chinese.

Refugees have come from all walks of life – high lamas, nomads, nobles and peasants. Many were forced to abandon their families to escape and a number were children, many of whom were orphans. The majority left Tibet with nothing and now faced all the difficulties of adapting to a strange culture and a different climate.

With banners flying, the Tibetan band marches down to the Dalai Lama's palace in Dharamsala, India, for the new year ceremonies. The Tibetans have kept their history and culture alive. Yet the children have received a progressive, modern education – computers included.

In dealing with the influx, the Indian Government showed and still shows the greatest generosity. Settlements and land were granted to the refugees in many parts of India. Once with permanent bases, the Dalai Lama and his government have been able to oversee projects to help the communities adapt, while retaining their Tibetan culture.

Long years in India

And, indeed, Tibetan refugees have been cited as some of the most successful ever. In the thirty years since the Dalai Lama's escape, help has been received from the international community. Schools have been set up where, for the first time in their history, children from all backgrounds now receive a full-time education. Handicraft schemes, making beautiful carpets and other traditional objects, have been established which provide work for skilled Tibetan men and women. Hospitals have been built and new monasteries founded. Here, at least, the Tibetans can still follow their religion in peace.

Tenzin Gyatso has continued with his religious studies and teachings – for this will always be the most important concern of His Holiness. He has also set about reforming the ponderous and often undemocratic machinery of the Tibetan government, in the hope of an eventual return to Tibet. Consequently, in 1963 he issued a new liberal and democratic constitution for Tibet because he realized that one of the causes of his country's tragedy was its failure to reform.

Old Tibet was gone forever, and nobody would want it to return in its exact form. The Dalai Lama had long realized that reforms – particularly to the landowning system – were very necessary. His point was, and is, that these reforms should be carried out by the Tibetan people themselves.

Ever since he was a boy poring over his atlas with Heinrich Harrer in Lhasa, Tenzin Gyatso has loved the idea of travel. During the long years of exile that ambition has been achieved. He has been invited to many different countries where people from all walks of life, religion, interest and creed have flocked to hear him speak. Many of the

At the time of the Chinese invasion, the guerrilla leader of this group was a brilliant monk, specially selected for advanced training. When he heard that his mother and sister had been killed by the Communists, he took up arms. His companion was one of the guerrillas who escorted His Holiness to safety. Although the Dalai Lama opposes all violence, he can understand why some of his people have resorted to it.

world's political and religious leaders have spent hours in deep discussion with the Dalai Lama.

His message is not, as you might expect, all about the woes of Tibet, although that experience is implicit in all that he says. Nor does he appeal only to Buddhists. Rather, he makes a universal appeal to all humanitarians. He teaches the idea of every person developing a sense of universal responsibility for all members of the human race irrespective of creed, race, sex or nationality.

His starting point is the recognition that all beings cherish happiness and do not want suffering. It then, he says, "becomes both morally wrong and pragmatically unwise to pursue only one's own happiness oblivious to the feelings and aspirations of all others who surround us as members of the same human family." This applies as much to nations as individuals. Greed and selfishness cause wars; compassion and understanding avoid and heal them.

Thoughts for the modern person

What comes through all the Dalai Lama's speeches and writings is a great clarity of thought and an underlying humility. Although having a clear attitude to right and wrong, he believes there are many paths to achieve this. *All* religions have their good points, *all* people, whether they are religious or not, appreciate love and compassion. He also warns against taking extreme positions.

While believing that many of the world's problems are caused by excessive materialism of the West, he doesn't advise abandoning it and retreating to a mountain top. Rather, the aim should be to find ways of incorporating materialism with spiritual progress.

Many people find the Dalai Lama's double role in politics and religion difficult to appreciate. Surely one will contaminate the other? But His Holiness believes that politics is a means to an end, a way of solving human problems. If politicians approach these problems with the right motives, there can be no contamination. If they have the wrong motives, it is they who are at fault. In other

Above: Guerrillas in the snowy vastness of their country.

Left: A pile of broken relics. Precious metals were melted for bullion. One thousand religious ornaments – some one thousand years old – were hacked down and burned.

words, politicians can be "dirty", politics are not.

In his trips abroad – to the U.S.A., Britain, Europe and Japan – the Dalai Lama strikes a refreshingly new note in his treatment of individual, religious and world affairs. He talks about issues and problems in a way quite unlike many people have heard before. He even manages to baffle the press – used to exiled leaders touring the world beating their own drum.

As one reporter wrote after his visit to the United States in 1980, "He was a politician free from the taint of politics; a religious leader free from the taint of sectarianism; a refugee free from the taint of self-pity – a Buddha maybe."

Toward world peace

In 1984, the Dalai Lama published "A Human Approach to World Peace", a pamphlet outlining in a simple and uncomplicated way his personal approach to world peace.

As with all his thinking, he does not begin by launching into sweeping global statements. Rather, his starting point is with the individual – you or I. His argument is that if we adopt a selfish approach to life and constantly try to use others for our own gain, we may achieve temporary benefits, but in the long run we will not succeed in finding even personal happiness, let alone world peace.

Inner peace, then, is the starting point, and only by every individual striving for it can we begin to seriously tackle the roots of wider conflicts.

In his pamphlet, Tenzin Gyatso lists four proposals which he regards as essential if human society is to become more compassionate, just and equal:

★ *universal humanitarianism is essential to solve global problems*

★ *compassion is the pillar of world peace*

★ *all world religions already stand for world peace in this way, and so are all humanitarians of whatever ideology*

★ *each individual has a universal responsibility to shape institutions to serve human needs*

By beginning to develop one's own humanitarian instincts, the Dalai Lama argues, it is a logical step to apply them to global problems. And indeed it is a necessity in a modern world which, through rapid technological advances and international trade, has become a significantly smaller place. To survive, we *have* to get on with one another.

Aggression, greed and competitiveness have been part of the make-up of human beings since time began – and many believe they always will be. However, such traits have become that much more dangerous in a world that now abounds with sophisticated modern weaponry, and the nightmare of nuclear destruction.

To counter this, the Dalai Lama believes we need to strive for "undiscriminating compassion" – that is, not just to those to whom you are attached, such as friends or family, but a "wider love that you can have even for someone who has done harm to you: your enemy". Developing such a sense of compassion also produces a "calmness" which is useful to everyone, but especially, the Dalai Lama thinks, "to those responsible for running national affairs, in whose hands lie the power and opportunity to create the structure of world peace".

In his pamphlet, His Holiness appeals for a greater sense of understanding between different religions, communities, nations and political systems. No one system or political ideology is better than any other, he argues, and indeed a variety is desirable and enriches us all. By appreciating this we can escape from the "us and them" attitude which has brought, and is still bringing, so many woes to the world.

His are not the usual thoughts of an exiled leader who has suffered the destruction of his culture and his people, and it is this that makes his words so powerful and so moving.

A crack in the door

The death of Mao Tse-tung in 1976 and the subsequent fall of his supporters – the Gang of Four – resulted in a new liberalization policy in China. This eventually touched Tibet, beginning with a

"He has the most beautiful smile, ... which will appear at the most unexpected moments.... It is one of those smiles that is like the sun breaking through, and if it is directed at you, you never forget it."
    Roger Hicks and Ngakpa Chogyam, from their biography, "Great Ocean".

The Dalai Lama speaking to a large audience in India soon after his exile. Over the years his growing role as an advocate of personal development as a means to world peace, was to take him to audiences all over the world.

public admission by the Chinese leaders of the complete mess they had made of the country.

Things would change, they said, and in order to prove their good intentions, they invited representatives of the Dalai Lama to visit Tibet and see for themselves. They also announced their willingness to talk to the Dalai Lama about his return to Tibet where some "suitable" post would be found for him in the administration.

Thus in 1979, 1981, 1982 and 1985, four special delegations of Tibetan refugees went on fact-finding missions to their homeland.

The first reaction of the delegates was one of profound shock at the appalling destruction they found. Everywhere they saw abandoned monasteries: of 3,500 monasteries and libraries, less than a hundred were left standing. Holy images had been broken and defaced. Priceless religious statues and ornaments had been melted down and sold in Peking. To the Tibetans, the sacrilege and rape of their religion was a far deeper humiliation than the vast financial loss.

Worse was the Chinese treatment of the Tibetan people, which today effectively runs on a system of apartheid. In the major cities the Chinese live in segregated compounds in subsidized housing with electricity, water and sewers. The Tibetans, on the other hand, have no basic amenities and receive all the worst food, clothing and medical care.

The delegates were shocked by the seeping colonization of Tibet by Chinese settlers. Xining, once a Tibetan frontier town with China and only a few miles from where Tenzin Gyatso was born, had become an almost totally Chinese city.

It is this overwhelming Chinese presence that the Tibetans fear will soon dominate the whole country. As one recent visitor said "Nearly everyone you see is Chinese and the odd Tibetan in the street reminded me of the fate of the Australian Aborigines – reduced to a tourist attraction in their own land." And indeed, in this part of Tibet that was what they had already become. Outside the gates of the great Tibetan Monastery of Kumbum, photographers awaited the coach loads of Chinese tourists who had their pictures taken wearing traditional Tibetan costume.

The delegates also heard stories of a more sinister aspect of the Chinese encroachment – the forced abortions and sterilization of Tibetan women.

In Lhasa, the holy city of the Dalai Lamas, the Chinese population would soon become the majority. The Chinese had taken over most of the traditional Tibetan jobs, like tailoring and shoe-making, as well as running most of the shops and small restaurants. Even the people selling offertory scarves to visitors to the temple were Chinese.

Chinese workers were – and still are – encouraged to come here by special concessions and deals, allowing them to earn up to two or three times as much as in China itself. By contrast, unemployment among Tibetans in Lhasa has continually been as high as 70%, with many being reduced to begging and scrounging off foreign tourists.

And of course everywhere in Tibet was the overwhelming presence of the Chinese Army – a quarter of a million strong.

Tibetan religious and national feeling

The delegations did find that some Chinese repression had been eased. Collectivization of the land had been abolished, as in other parts of China proper, and the peasants had been allowed to revert to barley cultivation, with the freedom to sell excess grain on the free market. Some Tibetan was now taught in schools and the restrictions on travel within Tibet had been loosened.

But most importantly, from the people's point of view, the ban on following their religion had been relaxed. A few monasteries were being repaired, and monks were once again tending the butter lamps at the holy shrines of what was left of the great monasteries of Tibet. Chinese officials, though, still kept a tight rein on all monastic activity, vetting those taking vows and restricting their number.

What really impressed the delegates was the extraordinary strength of the Tibetans' devotion to the Dalai Lama and the Buddhist religion – in spite of everything the Chinese had done to destroy it.

Above: Monks of Sera monastery are made to wear ordinary clothes.

Opposite above: Despite appearances of a return to normality in the bazaars of Lhasa, the sinister uniforms of China's People's Liberation Army are everywhere. Over a quarter of a million troops are stationed in Tibet, and they are there to overawe the Tibetan population – by force if necessary – as illustrated by their actions from 1987 to 1989.

Opposite below: The compulsory portrait of Chairman Mao in a monastery. The only remaining monasteries are preserved as tourist attractions.

Everywhere the delegates went they were mobbed by weeping crowds crying for the return of their Dalai Lama. Initially the Chinese authorities were taken aback at such displays of devotion and were worried by the strength of the support for the Dalai Lama in Tibet – which they thought they had stamped out. This was one reason why negotiations between the two sides reached deadlock.

Tourists

Tibet was to see another invasion in the years between 1984 and 1987 – by camera-toting Western tourists. One reason for opening up the country in this way was certainly to cash in on the money they brought, which might go some way to shoring up the Tibetan economy, so badly abused and mishandled in the past.

The Chinese may also have hoped that an overdose of Western culture would more effectively snuff out Tibetan nationalism and traditions than any years of oppression could – just as it has done in so many other parts of the world. In the long term they might have been right.

However, the immediate result was to fan the flames of Tibetan nationalism. Many of the first visitors had contacts with the refugees, were sympathetic to their cause, and were able to tell people about the Dalai Lama and the outside world. Their impressions were that the simmering resentment against Chinese rule and the inadequacies of the "reforms" to date was reaching boiling point.

Escalating violence

In October 1987, monks in Lhasa protesting at the arrest of one of their fellows, clashed head on with the Chinese security police. An ugly riot followed in which a number of Tibetans were shot dead and hundreds arrested. Unfortunately for the Chinese, they were unable to hush this up – as in the past – because the city was full of tourists. Indeed, two American doctors narrowly escaped arrest themselves by helping badly-injured Tibetans too frightened to attend hospital – where they certainly would have been arrested.

"I was taken handcuffed to the police station. I was thrown on the floor, and they stamped on my face repeatedly, beat me with an electric prod and kicked me in the chest. We were then stripped naked and three or four people continued to poke us with electric prods. We were told that as we opposed the Chinese we would be executed."

Young nuns beaten by Chinese police following the riots of March 1988, interviewed for British television, 1988.

The reaction of the Chinese was an immediate clampdown. Lhasa was saturated with police and troops and thousands more settlers were brought in. Secret film, smuggled out and shown on British television, exposed a policy of genocide – a cold-blooded attempt to wipe out Tibetans and everything they believed in.

More violent clashes erupted in 1988 and again in 1989 on the anniversary of the Dalai Lama's exile on March 10. Despite Chinese attempts to shrug off the violence as the work of a few agitators, it is clear to anyone who has visited Tibet in the last six years that this was a national protest. Its outbreak was only a matter of time and it is deepening.

Only by negotiating promptly with the Dalai Lama can Peking ward off the rising violence that may soon imperil every Chinese person in Tibet. For it is only the Dalai Lama who can neutralize Tibetan resentment and national feeling – and the Chinese know it.

Peace proposals

And the Dalai Lama is prepared to negotiate, and indeed make concessions. He is deeply concerned about the steady encroachment of Chinese settlers. As he says: "There is every danger that the entire Tibetan nation, with their own unique religious culture, will disappear. If the present situation remains, Tibetans will soon be a minority in their own country."

The essence of his "Five Point Peace Plan" put to the Chinese in 1987 is firstly, the demilitarization of Tibet, and in particular the removal of the nuclear missile bases situated there; and secondly an end to the settlement of the region by hundreds of thousands of Chinese. In return the Dalai Lama is prepared to concede defence and foreign affairs to the Chinese.

Some among the Tibetan community feel that the Dalai Lama's gentle stand amounts to a surrender. They demand a totally independent Tibet, and a minority would be prepared to wage a long guerrilla war to achieve it. However, as the Dalai Lama stresses, "the question of independence is now

The Dalai Lama meets children from both the Catholic and Protestant communities of Northern Ireland. Tolerance for other religions, tolerance for different views within a religion, tolerance for people with no religion, has always been the touchstone of His Holiness's philosophy – so long as all have a "good heart".

A Tibetan tapestry depicting a religious theme. Such works of art adorn every Tibetan temple and household, evoking feelings of peace and harmony with the world.

"The religion of the future will be a cosmic religion. It should transcend a personal God and avoid dogmas and theology. It should be based on a religious sense arising from the experience of all things natural and spiritual as a meaningful unity. Buddhism answers this description."

Albert Einstein.

---

simply unrealistic. Practical autonomy must come first otherwise the very survival of the Tibetan people is threatened."

Negotiation on both sides is crucial, and it is surely the moral duty of the Chinese to make concessions after years of killing and repression. There are also practical reasons why they should do so. After Tiananmen Square China, more than ever, needs to placate the international community.

More crucially, a real nightmare for Peking would be if escalating violence in Tibet were to spread to regions such as Mongolia and Xinjiang, inhabited by large numbers of China's sixty million minority peoples. For Tibet's foreign minister-in-exile has warned that despite the Dalai Lama's deep beliefs in non-violence, he will be unable to prevent some of his people resorting to violence.

The story of Tibet is one of the great tragedies of the twentieth century – and it is still going on to this day. It is a tragedy that the rest of the world

either knows nothing about or chooses to ignore. The one sign of recognition has been the world's most prestigious award for peace work – the 1989 Nobel Peace Prize.

And through it all comes the smiling face of the Dalai Lama, still calm and serene in spite of everything, and with a message for the world.

This is what he wrote as a finale for his essay on world peace:

Whenever I meet even a "foreigner", I have always the same feeling: "I am meeting another member of the human family."

This attitude has deepened my affection and respect for all beings. May this natural wish be my small contribution to world peace. I pray for a more friendly, more caring, and more understanding human family on this planet.

To all who dislike suffering; who cherish lasting happiness – this is my heartfelt appeal.

There are still thousands of young Tibetan men who leave their homeland to come to Dharamsala each year to become monks. Like most Buddhist monks, they spend many hours each day in deep meditation and study. They harm no one, carry no weapons, they just want to be allowed to live in peace and follow their beliefs.

The fact that the Chinese military have continued to hound and persecute the monks – and the gentle people of Tibet – for forty years, is the saddest part of the whole Tibetan tragedy. That, and the empty silence about it across the world.

Important Dates

1933	Death of the thirteenth Dalai Lama.
1935	Birth of Tenzin Gyatso – the fourteenth Dalai Lama.
1937	The Dalai Lama, at the age of two, is found by a search party from Lhasa.
1940	The fourteenth Dalai Lama is enthroned in Lhasa.
1946	Civil War begins between Nationalists and Communists in China.
1947	India becomes independent.
1949	Chinese Nationalists are defeated and The People's Republic of China is proclaimed.
1950	Oct 7: The Chinese invade Tibet. The Dalai Lama assumes full power at the age of fifteen. Tibet makes an appeal for help to the United Nations and it is rejected. The young Dalai Lama flees to Yatung on the Indian border.
1951	Dec: The Tibetans are forced to agree to the Seventeen Point Agreement which stated that Tibet would be annexed to China and would be occupied by Chinese troops. The Dalai Lama returns to Lhasa.
1952	The Dalai Lama's chief ministers are dismissed by the Chinese.
1953	Communist reforms are imposed on eastern Tibet.
1954	The Dalai Lama visits Peking.
1955	First revolts are reported in the east of Tibet.
1956	The Dalai Lama visits India.
1956-1959	The revolts continue in the east of Tibet. Eastern tribesmen move west toward Lhasa.
1958	The Dalai Lama, aged twenty-three, passes his *Geshé* degree.
1959	March 10: The Tibetan Uprising takes place in Lhasa. The Dalai Lama flees to India. The uprising is ruthlessly crushed. Full communist reforms are imposed in Tibet. The United Nations condemns the Chinese atrocities.
1960	The Dalai Lama establishes his government in exile at Dharamsala, North India.
1963	A new constitution for Tibet is issued by the Dalai Lama from Dharamsala.
1966	The beginning of the Cultural Revolution in China.
1967	The Dalai Lama, aged thirty-two, makes his first overseas tour to Japan and Thailand.
1973	The Dalai Lama's first European tour.
1979	The Dalai Lama's first visit to the United States. The first signs of a more liberal Chinese attitude to Tibet begin to show. The First Delegation of Tibetan refugees visits Tibet.

1981	The Second Delegation of Tibetan refugees visits Tibet. The Dalai Lama makes major tours of the U.K. and the U.S.
1982	The Third Delegation of Tibetan refugees visits Tibet. The Dalai Lama makes major tours of the Far East, U.S.S.R. and Europe.
1984	Tibet is opened up to individual western tourists. The Dalai Lama publishes "A Human Approach to World Peace".
1985	The Fourth Delegation of Tibetan refugees visits Tibet.
1987	The Dalai Lama formulates his Five Point Peace Plan, and is invited to address the U.S. Congress. Serious riots take place in Lhasa in October. Tibet is closed again to individual travellers.
1988	Mar: Further serious riots take place in Lhasa during the Prayer festival. China at last agrees to discuss the Dalai Lama's peace plan.
1989	Jan: The Dalai Lama's representatives meet Chinese representatives in Geneva. Oct: The Dalai Lama is awarded the Nobel Peace Prize.

Further Reading

Avedon, John: *In Exile from the Land of Snows* (Wisdom Publications, London, 1985) [an adult book but easy to read]

Gyatso, Geshe Kelsang: *Buddhism in the Tibetan Tradition: A Guide* (Routledge and Kegan Paul, London, 1984) [an adult book]

Hicks, Roger & Chogyam, Ngakpa: *Great Ocean – An Authorised Biography – The Dalai Lama* (Element Books, Great Britain, 1984) [an adult biography but easy to read and comprehensive]

Snelling, John: *Buddhism* (Wayland, Great Britain, 1986)

Glossary

Asylum: A safe place of shelter and support for people whose safety and well-being has been threatened in some way.

Bodhisattva: A saint or semi-divine being in Mahayana *Buddhism* who foregoes *nirvana* in order to save others. Bodhisattvas are worshipped as symbols of compassion. The Dalai Lama is a Bodhisattva.

Buddha: The word "Buddha" means "one who has reached his goal" and is therefore "the enlightened or awakened one". This goal is reached through *meditation* and is the achievement of special religious knowledge and magical powers. The first Buddha was called Siddharta Guatama and was born in 560 B.C. His teaching was aimed at ordinary men and women.

Buddhism: The religion that grew from the teaching of the first *Buddha*, Siddharta Guatama. Buddhism spread from India into Asia, China and Japan. There are two main types – Theravada and Mahayana. Tibetan Buddhism has special features. The central aim of Buddhism is to give a final release from suffering which it believes is the cause of all the unhappiness in the world. Suffering is caused by human desire for power, success, money and human comforts. Buddhism leads the follower to *enlightenment* and then to *nirvana*.

Capitalism: The system of society which emphasizes private money and possessions.

Communism: A theory of society by which all property is vested in the community

and work is organized for the common benefit; everybody earns the same wages regardless of the job they do. This is the system of government that the Chinese have.

De facto: Something which is actually taking place even though certain groups of people might try to deny it. e.g. Tibet's independence after 1912 is a fact even though the Chinese were still arguing about it.

Dictatorship: When a country is under the absolute rule of one person.

Dogmatism: A way of thinking which is based upon ideas and principles that have not been tested in any way.

Enlightenment: The realization of the truth of all existence which was first achieved by the *Buddha* at Bodh Gaya. It also refers to the passing into *nirvana*.

Exile: When a person is exiled from their own country they are banished and it is not safe for them to return. As a result they can be taken in by other countries who offer them refuge. The Dalai Lama has been in exile in India for thirty years.

Genocide: The deliberate destruction of an entire race. It is estimated that one million Tibetans have been killed during the Chinese occupation of Tibet and that there are as many as three times more Chinese in Tibet now than there are Tibetans.

Guerrilla: An independent person who carries out war activities even though not part of any army. Tibet does not have an army of its own but its people have risen up against the Chinese.

Humanitarian: A person who tries to influence the world into being kinder and more considerate to the human race.

Lama: A Tibetan religious leader, credited with magical powers.

Materialism: Importance is attached to material objects and material needs, interests and desires.

Meditation: The application of the mind to an idea or religious truth. It involves long periods of time spent sitting quietly and relaxing the mind and body.

Nirvana: The goal of life for followers of *Buddhism*. It is the spiritual state characterised by release form the cycle of *reincarnation* and reached through the extinction of desire.

Refugee: One who, following religious persecution or political troubles, looks for safety in a foreign country.

Reincarnation: Being born into another life after death. In Buddhism it is believed that all humans, depending on how well or badly they behave, speak and think, will be born into a better or worse life the next time.

Serfdom: The situation of being a serf or type of slave. In most examples the serf was "attached to the soil" which meant that if the master left, the serf could stay with the same plot of land.

Vandalism: The ruthless destruction of anything beautiful or valuable.

The Chinese military have brutally suppressed all non-violent protest attempts by the Tibetans. On December 10, 1988 the Chinese military police opened fire on peaceful demonstrators in Lhasa. Many monks were beaten and arrested (above). Some of their families and friends have never heard of them since.

"I would like to appeal to all leaders of the nuclear powers who literally hold the future of the world in their hands, to the scientists and technicians who continue to create these awesome weapons of destruction and to all the people at large who are in a position to influence their leaders: I appeal to them to exercise their sanity and begin to work at dismantling and destroying all nuclear weapons."

The Dalai Lama.

"The Chinese cannot reject world concern by angrily saying it is interference with China's internal affairs; the abuse and degradation of a people concerns us all."

*Simon Normanton, from
"Tibet. The Lost Civilization".*
